CONTENTS

IN THE BOOK

TO DOWNLOAD

Medium term plan

Activity sheet 1: Provocation

Activity sheet 2: Map of North and South America

Activity sheet 3: The travellers' itinerary

Activity sheet 4: World map with latitude and longitude

Activity sheet 5: Climate graphs for places in North and South America

Activity sheet 6: Climate types for places in North and South America

Activity sheet 7: The location of places in North and South America

PowerPoint 1

PowerPoint 2

HOW TO TEACH ABOUT THIS TOPIC

GETTING STARTED WITH SUPERSCHEMES

The following four pages provide you with an explanation of the geography rooted in this unit plus background information to give you the confidence to get started. The whole suggested unit is laid out in the medium term plan, which is followed by detailed lesson plans for two lessons (Lessons 1 and 3). Further ideas for developing the unit complete the book. This SuperScheme asks pupils to plan a trip that takes a group of travellers from the north of North America to the southernmost tip of South America. In planning an information pack for the travellers, pupils learn latitude and longitude and how this is related to climate and time zones, in the context of the Americas.

LEARNING OUTCOMES

Key geographical learning through this unit comprises the following four areas:

Understanding and knowledge

- understanding the significance of latitude, longitude, the Equator, the Northern and Southern Hemispheres, the Tropics of Cancer and Capricorn, the Prime Meridian and time zones
- understanding key aspects of climate types.

Locational knowledge

- using maps to locate environmental regions, key physical and human characteristics and places in North and South America
- locating lines of latitude and longitude, the Equator, the Northern and Southern Hemispheres, the Tropics of Cancer and Capricorn, the Prime Meridian and time zones.

Human and physical geography

- describing key aspects of climate types.

Geographical skills

- using maps, atlases, globes and digital/computer mapping to locate countries and recognise the places studied.

MAP AND ATLAS SKILLS

This unit focuses on North and South America as a context for developing the skills to use globes and atlases and understand key lines of latitude and longitude. You will need to have a set of atlases available, as well as globes and wall maps. Globes are the best way to show latitude and longitude, and if several inflatable globes are available pupils can explore these themselves. It is important to give the pupils exposure to different kinds of maps and atlases – physical maps, climatic zone maps, political maps and maps depicting continents – so they can see the Earth represented in different ways. You could also show the pupils different projections. The familiar Mercator projection shows what many pupils will assume is the correct size and shape of countries; the Peters projection may seem distorted, but is arguably more accurate in terms of their relative size. This will inevitably lead to a discussion about why we represent the Earth in different ways.

INTEREST AND CONTEXT

Pupils may already be familiar with aspects of North and South America – the Statue of Liberty; the Grand Canyon; the Amazon Rainforest; Rio de Janeiro; Machu Picchu. This is an opportunity to introduce them to alternative places and spaces over the two continents. Offering pupils multiple depictions of unfamiliar places will help them form rounded views rather than stereotypes.

Encourage pupils to share their first- or second-hand experiences of the Americas – they can bring artefacts into school, or collect news items about natural events such as hurricanes. Make the most of any sporting events that take place there: the 2016 Olympic and Paralympic Games in Rio de Janeiro, for example.

KEY GEOGRAPHICAL VOCABULARY

Hemisphere, Equator, Arctic Circle, Antarctic Circle, Tropic of Capricorn, Tropic of Cancer, latitude, longitude, meridian, prime meridian, climate, desert, polar, temperate, tropical.

ABOUT THIS TOPIC

Now that satellite navigation is easily accessible, often in the palm of your hand, navigating our way around the globe is simple. Underpinning satellite navigation is the system of latitude and longitude, developed and refined over centuries by scientists, mathematicians and astronomers. Latitude and longitude pinpoint every place on Earth in relation to the Equator and the Prime Meridian, and using latitude and longitude gives us a common language to describe the location of places and find our way without reference to vague or subjective landmarks.

LATITUDE

Latitude describes locations in terms of how far north or south they are from the Equator, which divides the Earth into the Northern and Southern Hemispheres. Lines of latitude are a series of imaginary horizontal lines circling the Earth, all running parallel to the Equator. The longest is the Equator. They decrease in length as they get nearer to the Poles. Latitude is measured in degrees, from 90°N (the North Pole) to 90°S (the South Pole). There are five major lines of latitude: the Equator at 0°, the Tropics of Cancer (23.5°N) and Capricorn (23.5°S) and the Arctic (66.5°N) and Antarctic Circles (66.5°S). The distance measured by 1° of latitude is approximately 113km.

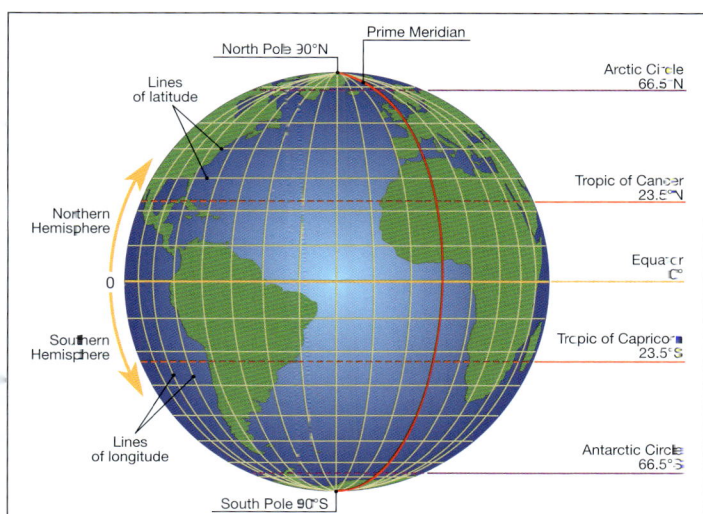

LONGITUDE

Lines of longitude are a series of imaginary vertical lines, all equal in length, that run from the North to the South Pole. They divide the Earth into segments, much like an orange. Longitude gives our position east or west of the Prime Meridian, which passes through the Royal Observatory in Greenwich, London. Longitude is measured in degrees, from 180°E to 180°W. On the opposite side of the Earth to the Prime Meridian is the International Date Line, which roughly follows 180° longitude through the Pacific Ocean (deviating around several island groups). The International Date Line divides one calendar day from the next. Going from west to east you lose a day; going from east to west you gain a day!

The Earth is divided into 24 standard meridians, at intervals of roughly 15° longitude, starting with the Prime Meridian. These meridians are the centre of 24 standard time zones (although some of these follow political boundaries). Time zones are related to the rotation of the Earth around the sun and ensure the maximum amount of daylight for the inhabitants of the zone. By standardising methods of time-keeping they also facilitate travel between zones.

LATITUDE AND CLIMATE

Climate is an average of weather conditions in a place over a 30-year period. Climate is affected by latitude, distance from the Equator, altitude and terrain. The hottest climates are near the Equator, where the sun's rays are most concentrated, and cooler towards the Poles, where the sun's rays are less concentrated as they are spread over a larger area (see diagram). Areas of the world with similar climates can be mapped as climate zones.

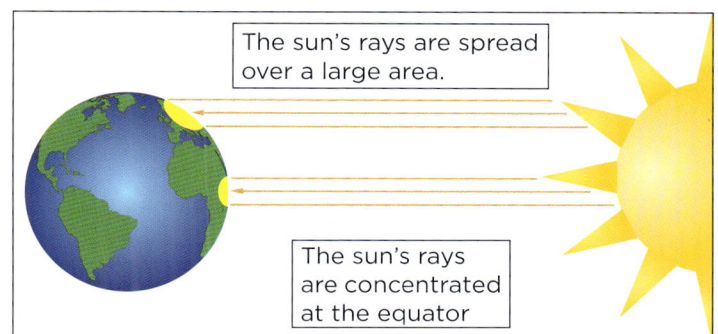

The sun's rays are spread over a large area.

The sun's rays are concentrated at the equator

MAIN CLIMATE TYPES

Equatorial climate

The sun's heat is most concentrated around the Equator, between the Tropics of Cancer and Capricorn. An equatorial climate is characterised by consistent temperatures (around 25-35°C), heavy rainfall, between 100mm-200mm/month, and high humidity (the amount of water vapour in the air). All of the world's tropical rainforests are in equatorial climates.

Tropical climate

The tropical climate has two very different seasons: hot summers with heavy rainfall (150-200mm/month) and a dry and very hot winter, with temperatures over 30°C. This climate has led to the growth of savannah, grassland with scattered trees and shrubs.

Hot desert climate

Areas of hot desert are located in the lower latitudes centred on the Tropics of Cancer and Capricorn. Deserts are found in areas of near-permanent high pressure that rarely produce rain. The temperature range is very wide, with high temperatures during the day and very low temperatures at night. Not all deserts are hot.

Temperate climate

Temperate climates describe a range of mid-level latitudes with variable temperature and rainfall. These areas have four distinct seasons: winters may fall below freezing, summers rise to 20°C. Rainfall is moderate, typically under 50mm/month.

Arctic and polar climates

In polar regions the sun's heat is least concentrated, making these the coldest places on Earth. They are also very dry. They have short wet summers, with temperatures from 1-10°C. The Arctic, because of the influence of the warmer Atlantic Ocean, is less cold than Antarctica, where temperatures can drop as low as –80°C.

LATITUDE, LONGITUDE AND NORTH AND SOUTH AMERICA

The continents of North and South America present a useful context for studying latitude, because they constitute an almost continuous landmass from 70°N to 55°S. This offers a wide range of climate types with varied ecosystems for pupils to explore.

The American continents cross many lines of longitude, from 40°W in Brazil to 170°W in Alaska, so they cover several time zones. In South and Central America there is a difference of three hours between the east and the west (Brazil is only three hours behind the UK). However there are four different time zones in the contiguous United States: the Eastern Time Zone is three hours ahead of the Pacific Time Zone on the west coast.

Bibliography

Dana, P.H. (2010) 'Longitude' in Warf, B. (ed) *Encyclopaedia of Geography*. Thousand Oaks, California: SAGE.

Fry, G.C. (1921) *Junior Geography*. London: University Tutorial Press.

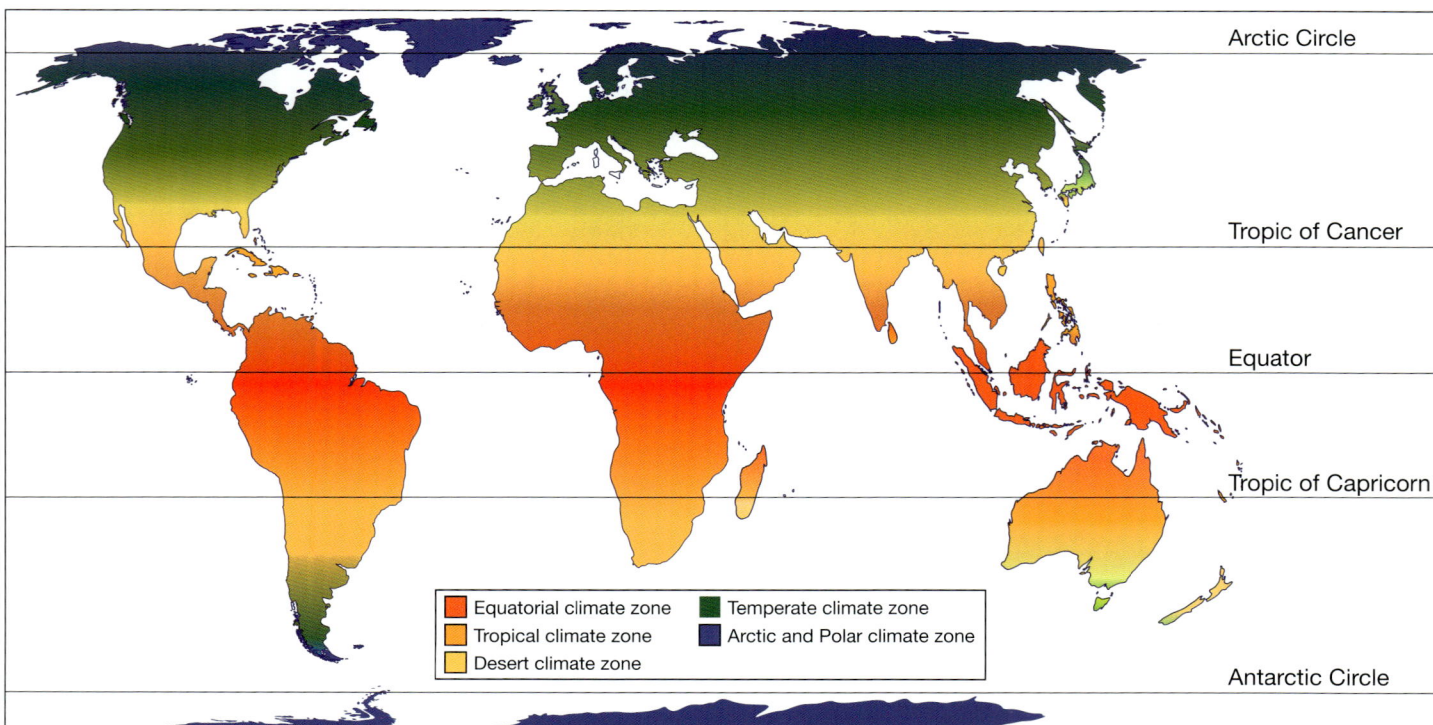

Legend: Equatorial climate zone · Tropical climate zone · Desert climate zone · Temperate climate zone · Arctic and Polar climate zone

Arctic Circle · Tropic of Cancer · Equator · Tropic of Capricorn · Antarctic Circle

Machu Picchu is one of the wonders of the Americas. This citadel built by the Incas stands at 2,400 metres above sea level in the Andes Mountains in Peru. Photo: John Royle.

Met Office (2012) 'Helping you understand Weather and Climate'. Available online at *www.metoffice.gov.uk/media/pdf/4/d/Weather_and_climate_guide.pdf* (last accessed 19 November 2015).

Pidwirny, M. (2006) *Map Location and Time Zones: Fundamentals of Physical Geography,* 2nd edition. Available online at *www.physicalgeography.net/fundamentals/2c.html* (last accessed 19 November 2015).

Schaffner, B. (2010) 'Blue Planet Biomes: World Climate Zones'. Available online at *www.blueplanetbiomes.org/climate.htm* (last accessed 19 November 2015).

Weisstein, E.W. (2007) 'Time Zone'. Available online at *http://scienceworld.wolfram.com/astronomy/TimeZone.html* (last accessed 19 November 2015).

Useful websites

BBC Nature: Places *www.bbc.co.uk/nature/places*
Discover USA *www.discoveramerica.com*
Essential Costa Rica *www.visitcostarica.com*
Keep Exploring *www.canada.travel*
National Geographic's 'Canada's 50 Places of a Lifetime' *http://travel.nationalgeographic.com/travel/canada/places-of-a-lifetime*
www.geography.org.uk/resources/mappingourglobe looks at some of the basic principles of creating and using world maps.

Amazing Americas!

Hundreds of polar bears come every autumn to the frozen shores of Hudson Bay in Manitoba to hunt for ringed seals.

Temperatures in the Mojave Desert in California can reach 51°C, and it receives only 5cm of rain a year.

Costa Rica is 129th in the world in terms of size but home to 5% of the Earth's biodiversity. Conservation areas cover 25% of the country. The forests are home to jaguars, sloths and monkeys.

The Amazon rainforest, at around 5.5 million square kilometres, is the largest tropical rainforest in the world, home to 10% of all species identified by science.

1000 kilometres off the coast of mainland Ecuador are the Galapagos Isles, home to the isolated ecosystems that Charles Darwin studied when formulating his theory of the origin of the species.

The Andes mountain range provides a habitat to different animals and vegetation that have adapted to cold and difficult conditions.

At the southernmost tip of South America, in the Tierra del Fuego, glaciers flow to the sea and many penguin rookeries can be found.

MEDIUM TERM PLAN

Lesson	Learning outcomes	Key questions	Pupil activities
1: Introducing North and South America	To use maps to locate places in North and South America To become familiar with the geography of North and South America	What places do we know in North and South America? How do we use the atlas to find where places are?	The class is given the provocation on **Activity sheet 1** asking them to design a trip from the northernmost part of North America and finishes at the southernmost tip of South America. Pupils have to identify places to visit. Use the images on **PowerPoint 1** as a starter. After drawing up a class list, pupils select six places either for one of the two groups of travellers on **Activity sheet 1** or for a generic trip. Pupils locate their final list of six places on the map in **Activity sheet 2** using the success criteria on PowerPoint 1 and complete the appropriate columns on **Activity sheet 3.**
2: Finding latitude and longitude	To find the latitude and longitude of places	What is latitude? What is longitude? Why is it useful to know the longitude and latitude of a location?	Use a globe or an atlas to discuss lines of latitude and longitude. Use the world map (**Activity sheet 4)** to locate the place where you live and model how to work out the longitude and latitude. Pupils practise this by finding the latitude and longitude of where the travellers from **Activity sheet 1** live. Label these on **Activity Sheet 4**. Pupils use an atlas to find the latitude and longitude of the places they have selected for their trip and complete the appropriate column on **Activity sheet 3**. Play a globe tossing game.
3: Linking latitude and climate	To identify patterns in climate data To explore the relationship between latitude and climate To understand the significance of latitude	What pattern does the climate graph show? How do the climate graphs compare? Why does climate vary with latitude?	Discuss the statement 'The further south you travel, the warmer the climate'. Using **PowerPoint 2** and **Activity sheet 5**, introduce the five climate graphs. Pupils describe the graphs and match them with the places on **Activity sheet 6**, and marking their location on the map on **Activity sheet 7**. Pupils find the climate of the places they are visiting and complete the appropriate column on **Activity sheet 3**. Demonstrate the link between latitude and climate using an inflatable globe and a torch and the diagram on **PowerPoint 2**. Reinforce understanding using the BBC Class Clip.
4: Linking longitude and time	To calculate time differences To understand the relationship between longitude and time zones	Why is it 3 p.m. in London and 10 a.m. in New York? Why do you think the world is organised into time zones? What is the Prime Meridian and where is it?	Discuss what makes day and night. Relate this to longitude, meridians and time zones from **Lesson 2**. Ask pupils what time it is in New York now. Refer back to the world map from **Activity sheet 4** in **Lesson 2** and use an atlas or time zone map from the internet to calculate the time at each of the places at the travellers' homes when it is mid-day in New York. Pupils could then calculate when they would have to set off in order to arrive in New York before mid-day, when the trip starts. Which traveller has the longest journey, and which order do they need to set off in to reach New York by mid-day? Show pupils a time zone map of North and South America. Pupils complete the time zone section on **Activity sheet 3**.
5: Applying knowledge of latitude and longitude	To present information clearly and attractively To apply an understanding of latitude, longitude, time zones and climate	What information will the travellers find most helpful? How can I present the information effectively?	Pupils create an information pack for the travellers as outlined in **Activity sheet 1**. They will need to draw on the information they have gathered on **Activity sheet 3**. They will need to research the places they have chosen to visit. **Activity sheet 1** gives the success criteria for the information pack. The information pack could be in the form of a leaflet, a poster, a PowerPoint presentation or some other format. It needs to include a map showing the location of each place.
6: Evaluating each other's work	To evaluate work against success criteria for the trip through the Americas	How have the success criteria been met?	Pupils present their work to the rest of the class. Pupils peer-mark each other's work against the success criteria from **Activity sheet 1**. This could be a mark out of 5 or traffic lights. Have a class discussion about which piece of work met the brief the most successfully? Why? Pupils decide which trip they would go on and why.

Resources	Assessment opportunities
Activity sheet 1: Provocation	Can the pupils locate places in an atlas?
Activity sheet 2: Maps of North and South America	Can pupils label the blank map of North and South America?
Activity sheet 3: The travellers' itinerary	
PowerPoint 1	
Atlases	
Google Earth	
Activity sheet 1: The provocation	Can pupils give the latitude and longitude of where they live?
Activity sheet 2: Maps of North and South America	Can pupils give the latitude and longitude of their chosen places in North and South America?
Activity sheet 3: The travellers' itinerary	
Activity sheet 4: World map with latitude and longitude	
Atlases	
Inflatable globe	
Activity sheet 5: Climate graphs for places in North and South America	Can pupils describe the temperature and rainfall pattern on a climate graph?
Activity sheet 6: Climate types for places in North and South America	Can pupils match the climate graph to the description of the climate type?
Activity sheet 7: The location of places in North and South America	
PowerPoint 2	
Inflatable globe	
Torch	
BBC Class clip 'Climate zones across the globe'	
Activity sheet 4: World map with latitude and longitude	Can pupils calculate the time difference between places?
Atlases	Can pupils calculate what time the travellers would have to set off to arrive in New York by mid-day?
Time zone/meridian map from the internet	
Activity sheet 1: Provocation	
Activity sheet 3: The travellers' itinerary	
Activity sheet 1: Provocation	How have the pupils' information packs met the success criteria?
	Have pupils demonstrated an understanding of latitude and longitude?

LESSON 1: INTRODUCING NORTH AND SOUTH AMERICA

LEARNING OUTCOMES

- to use maps to locate places in North and South America
- to become familiar with the geography of North and South America.

RESOURCES

- Activity sheet 1: Provocation
- Activity sheet 2: Maps of North and South America
- Activity sheet 3: The travellers' itinerary
- PowerPoint 1
- Atlases
- Google Earth

BACKGROUND

The Muddy Footprints adventure travel company wants your pupils to plan a trip that takes a group of travellers from the north of North America to the southernmost tip of South America, and to prepare an information pack for the travellers. As you work through the unit, pupils will acquire the skills and knowledge they need to complete the information pack, which engages their sustained interest and gives them a problem to solve.

The focus of this lesson is the geography of North and South America. The pace of learning will depend on pupils' prior knowledge; asking them what they already know about these continents is a good opportunity to address any misconceptions and build on their place knowledge.

INTRODUCTION

Show the class the video clip on **PowerPoint 1**. Brainstorm all the places pupils know in North and South America. Talk about the practicalities of adventure travel – what forms of transport do they think would be best? What kind of person do they think would choose this sort of holiday? How long do they think it would take? Give pupils **Activity sheet 1**, setting out the background to the task and introducing two groups of people who have already signed up for the trip. This can lead on to a discussion about which places these travellers might want to visit.

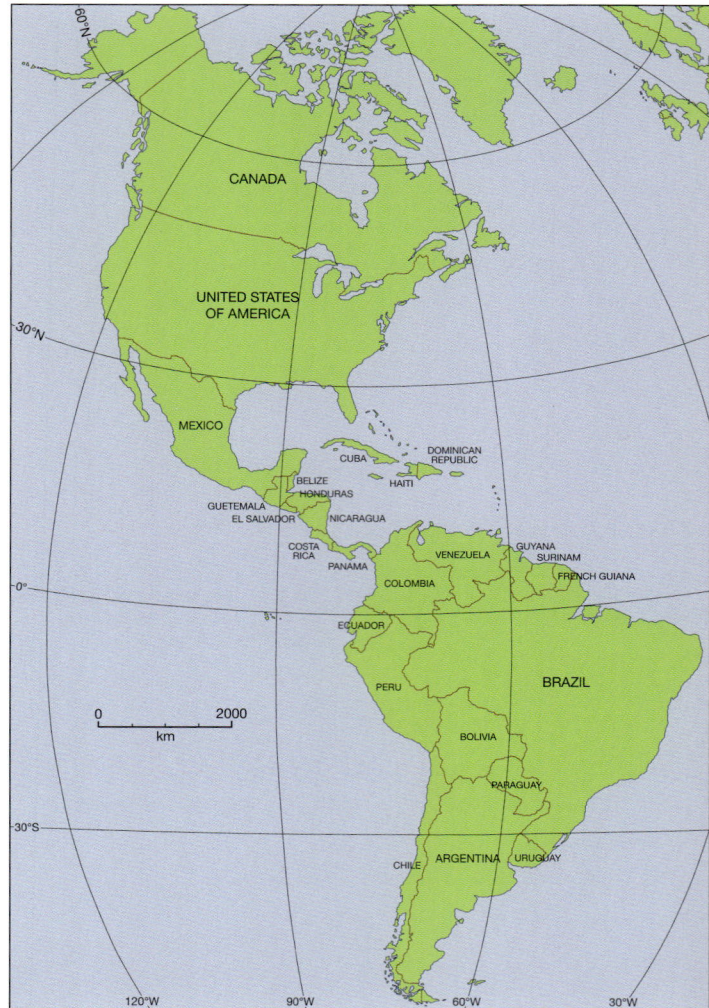

MAIN TASK

The main lesson activity is to identify suitable places in North and South America for the travellers to visit. This could be a generic list, or tailored to the two groups of travellers. Begin by locating North and South America, using atlases and the map of North and South America on **PowerPoint 1**. Explain that a continent is a group of countries on a continuous expanse of land, and ask pupils where North America and South America begin and end. Make sure that they can distinguish between North America (the continent) and the USA (the country). Brainstorm different countries in North America, then South America. You can use Google Earth to 'zoom in' to different places in North and South America.

Pupils can compile their lists in pairs or small groups, or individually. The advantage of group or paired work is that the pupils can work in the same groups or pairs subsequently to create their presentation. Ask them to choose places in both North and South America, some with natural features and others with human features. If they have difficulty getting started, you can show them the photographs on **PowerPoint 1**. Combine the pupils suggestions into a class list and ask them as a class to choose the six best places.

Using the blank map on **Activity sheet 2**, pairs of pupils locate the six places, along with the northernmost and southernmost points. There are a range of maps; some pupils may also be able to label countries, seas and oceans others could use the maps with the countries a ready labelled. The maps also show latitude and longitude, this will be the focus in lesson 2.

The success criteria below (also on **PowerPoint 1** to display to the class) set out how to use an atlas to locate a place on a blank map. You may want to model it and make a mistake for the pupils to spot (and gloat over!)

How to use an atlas to locate a place on a blank map

- find the place in an atlas (using the index if necessary)
- find nearby features and landforms (e.g. the shape of the coastline or the country border)
- identify the same features and landforms on your blank map
- mark the place on your blank map.

If pupils are working in pairs or small groups, make sure they do the atlas work individually, or take it in turns, so all pupils get the chance to develop their geographical skills and understanding. If school atlases do not include all the places you think pupils will come up with, you could also use an online map or Google Earth.

PLENARY

Rather than a single plenary at the end of the lesson, you may want to use mini-plenaries throughout. As you work with the class, you may encounter misconceptions, problems or particularly good examples, and you may want to pause the lesson to discuss them. You can ask the class to respond to each other's opinions, and use good examples to reinforce how to achieve the learning objective. This will also support any pupils who are finding the lesson difficult. Pupils can enter their final list of six places on **Activity sheet 3**; the other information required for **Activity sheet 3** can be compiled as you work through the following lessons.

PROGRESSION

To add a challenge, pupils could plan a bespoke adventure for one of the two groups of travellers, or they could suggest their own group of travellers and design a trip for them.

LESSON 3: LINKING LATITUDE AND CLIMATE

LEARNING OUTCOMES

- to identify patterns in climate data
- to explore the relationship between latitude and climate
- to understand the significance of latitude.

RESOURCES

- Activity sheet 5: Climate graphs for places in North and South America
- Activity sheet 6: Climate types for places in North and South America
- Activity sheet 7: The location of places in North and South America
- PowerPoint 2
- Inflatable globe
- Torch
- BBC Class clip 'Climate zones across the globe': www.bbc.co.uk/learningzone/clips/climate-zones-across-the-globe/11182.html

BACKGROUND

The continents of North and South America, covering an almost continuous landmass from 70°N to 55°S, offer a wide range of climate types to explore. This lesson covers a lot of subject knowledge: pupils will be introduced to five different climate types and will learn how latitude affects climate. You may need to allow plenty of time in the concluding discussion for all pupils to ask questions about how the distribution of the sun's rays on the curved surface of the Earth affects climate.

INTRODUCTION

Remind pupils about the travellers in Lesson 1, embarking on their journey from New York then travelling from the north of North America to the southernmost tip of South America. The travellers will want to know what weather they will experience and what clothes and equipment to pack. Open the discussion with this statement: 'The further south you travel, the warmer the climate'. Make sure pupils know what 'climate' means by asking them to describe the weather where they live – how does the weather alter over the course of the year? You can then make the distinction between weather (which can change from day to day) and climate (the average rainfall and temperature over

30 years). Discuss with the class the main variants in climate types – rainfall and temperature.

During the lesson, display the map of the Americas from PowerPoint 2 for pupils to refer to: this will help them back up their responses with evidence, and will give you an idea of what they already know so you can adjust the rest of your lesson accordingly. If they give simple yes or no answers, you could challenge them with another question or a contradictory fact (e.g. what about Antarctica? Is Mexico warmer than Brazil?)

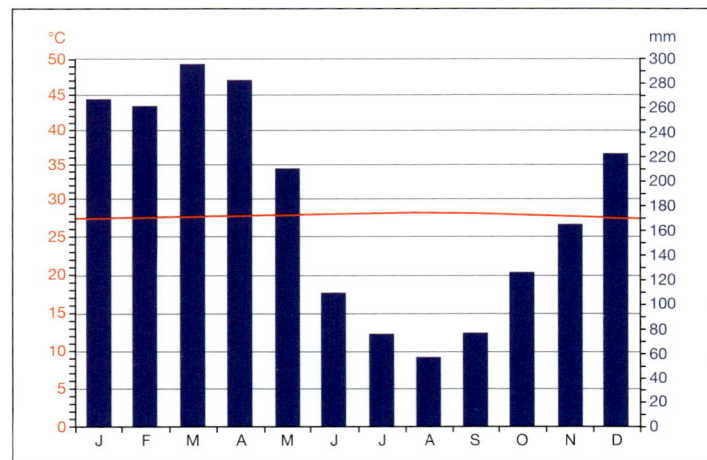

Manaus (latitude 3°S), in the Amazon rainforest of Brazil, has an equatorial climate, with high temperatures throughout the year and high rainfall.

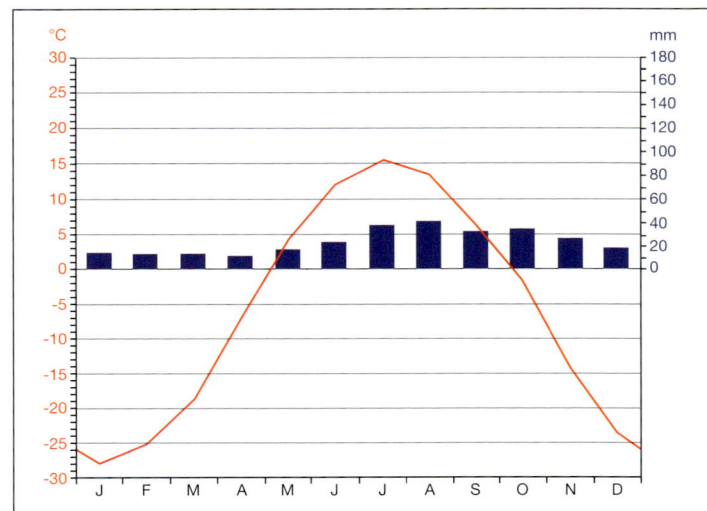

Yellowknife (latitude 62°N) in the tundra of Canada, has a polar climate, with low rainfall and winter temperatures well below freezing.

MAIN TASK

Introduce the class to the climate graphs on **PowerPoint 2** and discuss what it would be like to live in each place: How does the temperature change throughout the year? Is the rainfall high or low? Does the rainfall change throughout the year? If the travellers visit during our summer, July-August, what weather would they be likely to experience? This is a good opportunity to draw attention to the climate graphs for the Southern Hemisphere, where summer is experienced during December and January.

Give pupils **Activity sheet 5**, which asks them to describe the patterns they observe in the rainfall and temperature graphs, and **Activity sheet 6**, for which they have to match descriptions of places to the corresponding climate graph. The success criteria below, (also on **PowerPoint 2** to display to the class) set out how to look for patterns in a climate graph and match it to a climate type.

How to identify climate types from climate graphs

- look at the temperature on the graph (this is shown by a line graph)
- look at the rainfall shown on the graph (this is shown by a bar graph)
- think about how to describe the pattern shown on the graph
- look at the numbers on the axes of the graph, what does this tell you about how hot or cold the place is and the amount of rainfall?
- match the pattern to the description of the different climate types.

Finally, **Activity sheet 7** asks them to locate the places on **Activity sheet 6** on a map of North and South America. Use prompting questions to help them link the graphs, the descriptions and the map. The answers can be found on **PowerPoint 2**, along with photos illustrating each place. Pupils could stick large versions of the graphs onto a wall map.

Draw attention to the latitude for each place on **Activity sheet 6** and recap what they have learned about latitude in the previous lesson. Pupils find the climate of the places they are visiting on their planned journey. They complete the climate section on **Activity sheet 3**.

CONCLUDING DISCUSSION

Rather than a plenary, this is an opportunity for pupils to make the link between latitude and climate. Ask them what patterns they can see on their map. How does the temperature change with latitude? Is there a pattern with rainfall? Prompting them to use evidence, give the class some time to think about why this might be.

Then display the diagram on the final slide of **PowerPoint 2** and use an inflatable globe and a torch to model how sunlight is distributed differently at the Equator and at the Poles. This affects the way air moves around the globe and how bodies of water are heated, which in turn affects the climate. You can show the BBC Class Clip to reinforce pupils' understanding of the different climate types and their location.

PROGRESSION

Pupils could find out more information about these five places. What is life like there? What sort of vegetation do they have? They could use weather websites such as BBC Weather to find today's temperature in these locations.

A popular activity for tourists in Punta Arenas (Graph D on Activity sheet 5) is to take a short boat trip to the nature reserve on the small and rocky Magdelena Island where thousands of penguins breed. Photo: Luis Alejandro Bernal Romero http://aztlek.com

DEVELOPING THE UNIT

Lesson 2: Finding latitude and longitude

- Pupils write a song or a poem or acrostic explaining what latitude and longitude is.

- Pupils find the latitude and longitude of places in the UK.

- Pupils make a treasure map of the ocean with lines of latitude and longitude. They have to find the treasure that is hidden in a shipwreck at the bottom of the ocean.

- Play a globe tossing game when a pupil catches the globe they have to give the latitude and longitude of the place that is under the middle finger of their right hand.

Examples of resources

Mr M and Mr Parker sing about the importance of latitude and longitude to the tune of One Direction's 'You don't know you're beautiful': *www.youtube.com/watch?v=5Ab-gE8ov4o*

At iTouchMap you can click on a point on a map and it will tell you the latitude and longitude: *http://itouchmap.com/latlong.html*

ABCYA offer a longitude and latitude treasure hunt game which helps pupils to practise their skills: *www.abcya.com/latitude_and_longitude_practice.htm*

There are lots of teaching ideas for using an inflatable globe in your geography lessons, to download from the GA website *www.geography.org.uk/shop/shop_detail.asp?ID=655*

Lesson 4: Linking longitude and time

- Start a discussion about day and night by talking about what children are doing in different parts of the world, are they in bed? at school? at home in the evening?

- Pupils calculate the time in a range of places using a time zone convertor or the world clock app on ipads and smart phones.

- Put several clocks on the classroom wall with the times for different places, e.g. Sydney, Mumbai, New York. Label each clock with the place and its longitude.

Examples of Resources

The Black Marble + Earth at Night: *www.youtube.com/watch?v=iPLknomVxRc*

NASA eClips has a really informative discussion of longitude and time zones: *www.youtube.com/watch?v=kDWHM00sZJc*

Time zone converters are freely available on the Internet: *www.timeanddate.com/worldclock/converter.html*

Time zone map: *www.timetemperature.com/time-zone-maps/large-world-time-zone-map.shtml*

Adler, D. A. (2010) *Time Zones.* New York: Holiday House. This entertaining book explains why time zones exist and other interesting facts.

Lesson 5: Applying knowledge of latitude and longitude

- Select some examples of tourist brochures from your local train station or tourist information office to stimulate discussions about how to present information.

- Pupils could make postcards from places they visit including an image of each place, its latitude and longitude and details about the climate.

- Make a 'latitude and longitude' souvenir, such as a poster or bracelet, for each place you visit.

Examples of resources

BBC Skillswise gives suggestions on how to present information clearly: *www.bbc.co.uk/skillswise/factsheet/en38pres-e3-f-presenting-information*

Products with ideas for latitude and longitude souvenirs: *www.etsy.com/uk/market/latitude_longitude*

Lesson 6: Evaluating each other's work

- Get different groups of pupils to make a 'Dragons' Den'-type pitch for their trip, to the rest of the class or some 'Dragons' such as the head teacher, a governor, etc.

Examples of Resources

These titles demonstrate how to conduct peer-evaluation exercises, with examples:
Clarke, S. (2014) *Outstanding Formative Assessment: Culture and Practice.* London: Hodder Education.
Clarke, S. (2008) *Active Learning through Formative Assessment.* London: Hodder Education.